# ST. THOMAS
# AND THE GREEKS

6710

PRINTED AT THE MARQUETTE UNIVERSITY PRESS
MILWAUKEE, WISCONSIN

*The Aquinas Lecture, 1939*

# SAINT THOMAS

## AND

# THE GREEKS

Under the Auspices of the Aristotelian Society
of Marquette University

BY *Charles*

### ANTON C. PEGIS

*1905-*

*Fellow of the Institute of Mediaeval Studies,
Assistant Professor of Philosophy, Fordham
University Graduate School*

SECOND PRINTING

*39-23515*

MARQUETTE UNIVERSITY PRESS
MILWAUKEE
1943

MARQUETTE UNIVERSITY PRESS

MILWAUKEE

TO
REV. GERALD B. PHELAN
PRESIDENT, INSTITUTE OF MEDIAEVAL
STUDIES, TORONTO

## Nihil Obstat

Gerard Smith, S.J., censor deputatus
Milwaukiae, die 28 Julii, 1939


## Imprimatur

Milwaukiae, Die 16 iunii, 1939
+ Samuel A. Stritch
Archiepiscopus Milwaukiensis

# THE AQUINAS LECTURES

The Aristotelian Society of Marquette University each year invites a scholar to speak on the philosophy of St. Thomas Aquinas. These lectures have come to be called the Aquinas Lectures and are customarily delivered on the Sunday nearest March seven, the feast day of the Society's patron saint.

This year the Aristotelian Society has the pleasure of recording the lecture of Anton C. Pegis, Ph.D., assistant professor of philosophy in the Fordham University Graduate School, New York, N. Y.; B.A., M.A., Marquette University; Ph.D., University of Toronto, Carnegie Fellow, St. Michael's College, University of Toronto; Fellow of the Institute of Mediaeval Studies, University of Toronto; Instructor in Philosophy, Marquette University, 1932-1934; Assistant Professor of Philosophy, Marquette University, 1934-1937; Assistant Professor of Philosophy, Fordham University, 1937—; Assistant Editor of *New Scholasticism;* Member of American Catholic Philosophical Association and Mediaeval Academy of America; Author of: *St. Thomas and the Problem of the Soul in the 13th Century* (Toronto, 1934); Contributor to *New Scholasticism, Proceedings of the American Catholic Philosophical Association, Speculum* and *Thought;* Aquinas Lecturer, Marquette University, 1939.

# St. Thomas and the Greeks

## I

ST. THOMAS AQUINAS is studied and interpreted from so many different points of view, and there are such varying appreciations of his significance, that it ought not to be necessary to apologize for any attempt to reach the living historical personality from which all these interpretations are distilled. Such an undertaking, however, may seem strange to those who, living in the twentieth century, are frankly not interested in the thirteenth century and its complicated intellectual life, even when they are very much interested in the philosophical ideas of the Angelical Doctor. Such an undertaking may seem strange also to those who will wonder why it should receive the title of the present lecture. In both instances my apology is one and the same. If it is true that the ideas of St. Thomas Aquinas have a perennial value, it is not by ignoring or forgetting the intellectual world in which they came into being that we shall give them such a value. On the contrary, they rise above that world to an atemporal realm of truth by successfully mastering its problems. Angel of the Schools though he may be, St. Thomas does not speak from some abstract philosophical heaven. It is to the thirteenth century that St. Thomas gives voice—to that century, precisely, which was the first Christian century to behold and to feel the full power of the Greek philosophical genius. In the following lecture, it will be my purpose to suggest that the real significance of St. Thomas Aquinas is not seen until it is viewed in the astonishingly turbulent intellectual life of his century, and that when St. Thomas is so viewed, his relations to the Greeks and their Arabian successors assume the role of a major issue in the formation of his thought.

The thirteenth century was the age in which Christian thinkers were confronted with the enormous literature of Greek and Arabian philosophy. The special significance of this historical circumstance lies in this, that up to the time when they came into contact with Greek and Arabian ideas, Christian thinkers were ignorant not simply of the philosophical speculations of Greek and Arabian thinkers, they were also ignorant of the nature and structure of philosophical thinking. The thirteenth century is thus not simply the age in which Christians first came into contact with the completely formed philosophical systems of an Aristotle or an Avicenna. This is true, but it is only part of the truth. It is also true that up to this time Christian thinkers had still to formulate for themselves the very notion of philosophy and of philosophical knowledge. No doubt, there were philosophical ideas and principles in the speculations of early mediaeval thinkers. But until we come to the thirteenth century, the question as to the nature of philosophy, as distinguished from religious knowledge or from the meditations of a Christian reason on the content of an equally Christian revelation, was not asked. The problem of faith and reason in early mediaeval thought remains primarily a disciplinary one, and is not concerned with distinguishing philosophy from theology or knowledge from belief. It is this fact which gives to the thought of an Eriugena or a St. Anselm the apparent daring that it has. Far from even pretending to rationalism, they have still to learn the meaning of the philosophical use of reason: their intellectual lives move evenly within the realm of religious symbolism. In the twelfth century, Alain of Lille, a poet of considerable talent, as well as a theologian, expressed in a line an idea that may be taken as the model of early mediaeval thought in general: *quod lingua nequit, pictura fatetur* [1]. But the philosophical tongue which remains so much in ignorance of itself, and which is replaced by meditation and symbolism, biblical as well as mythological, becomes articulate with the thirteenth century. Beginning with this century, Christian thinkers were called upon not only to continue the traditions of early mediaeval speculation, not only to incorporate within

these traditions the new non-Christian philosophical literature that began to be translated
in Spain before the middle of the twelfth century, but also to learn to speak the language
of philosophy in order to meet this invasion
by the philosophers. Only, Christian thinkers
were forced to borrow from their adversaries
their very weapons of defense.

The two processes of discovering Greek
and Arabian philosophy and of learning to
discuss philosophical problems in a philosophical way, are inseparably related one to the
other. Hence, the attitudes which thirteenth
century thinkers adopted towards Plato, Aristotle, Avicenna, Averroes, not to mention a
host of other Greek and Arabian philosophers, were an index of their view on the
nature of philosophy itself. The different
philosophical movements that dominated the
thirteenth century are not simply historical
phenomena, more or less accidental to the
nature of philosophy; they are the channels
through which mediaeval thinkers expressed

their convictions as to the nature and place of philosophy within a Christian world. *How* a thirteenth century thinker understood and evaluated the philosophy of Aristotle, for example, was not for him, and should not be for us, an historical exercise; in such an understanding and evaluation there was also contained the problem of what philosophy itself was.

We must not forget this complicated historical situation in which philosophy came into existence in a Christian world. We must not forget it when we study either the history of mediaeval thought from the thirteenth century and after, or the thought of any particular mediaeval thinker during this same period. How such a thinker appreciated the events that were going on around him could mean also, and did mean, how he evaluated the nature of philosophy. In the presence of so many Greek and Arabian prophets of philosophy it is easy to see that unexpected dangers awaited Christian thinkers. That is, it is easy for the historian to see this, for the historian possesses that strange advantage of prophesying facts after they happen. But it is true that they did happen, and it is true that more than one Christian thinker became embarrassed as a philosopher as well as a Christian believer because of the way in which he chose his philosophical company.

Early and late in his career, St. Thomas was concerned with this problem of the reception of Greek and Arabian philosophy into a Christian world. This is so true that very soon he found himself in the anomalous position of being suspected both by those who wished to have nothing to do with pagan philosophers and by those who were surrendering more or less completely to the philosophical charms of these same pagans. The suspicions of his contemporaries were well founded. St. Thomas agreed neither with those who, to use the caustic words of Robert Greathead, Bishop of Lincoln, were making themselves heretics in the process of trying to make Aristotle a Catholic [2], nor with those who turned their back on philosophy in order to avoid the errors of the philosophers. Loyal as he was to Aristotle, St. Thomas never conceded that the Stagirite was incarnate philosophical truth or that Averroes was his prophet. Nor, on the other hand, did he concede to those Christian theologians who had learned from St. Augustine to mistrust the human reason and who looked upon the contemporary errors of philosophers as a confirmation of their mistrust, the right to deprive man of his dignity as a creature in order to add to his dignity as a Christian.

The relations of St. Thomas Aquinas to Greek philosophy and to the Arabian thinkers who were its heirs are inseparable from his relations to his contemporaries. The more he studied Greek and Arabian thought, the more he became convinced that a misunderstanding of the fundamental principles of this thought could prove and, indeed, was proving, disastrous to Christian thinkers. At least, the occupation of St. Thomas Aquinas with the ideas of Greek and Arabian Neoplatonism was intended as an historical and philosophical lesson which he and his contemporaries had to learn if they were to assimilate successfully and without calamity the philosophical ideas of their Greek and Arabian masters. The problem of the relations between St. Thomas and the Greeks, therefore, is as much a problem of immanent criticism in the thirteenth century as it is a problem in the relations between a thinker of the thirteenth century and his ancient Greek predecessors. It was an immediate problem for the thirteenth century to be occupied with the reception of Greek and Arabian ideas; it became an immediate problem for St. Thomas Aquinas to determine the nature of these ideas in order to determine their status and their suitability within a Christian world. Could one philosophize after the manner of Plato and still be a Christian?

If this question appears ambiguous or even naive, let me state it in a different way. We can grant that the Plato who wrote the *Republic* or even the *Timaeus* expressed himself in a way which was sufficiently mythical and dramatic in order not to demand of us too explicit a metaphysical faith as to the ultimate nature of reality [2a]. The idea of the Good is shrouded in metaphor and the story of the origin of the universe is a tale only approximately true. But Plato had, sooner or later, to give a rational defense of the vision which Socrates held up so persuasively before the young eyes of Glaucon and Adeimantus, and which Plato himself saw with impassioned gaze beyond the dramatic machinery of the dialogues. Unlike some of his interpreters, Plato was not satisfied with vague absolutes. The Plato who wrote the *Parmenides* and the *Sophistes* made such an examination and defense of his own metaphysical faith; and the theory of being which he established in these dialogues is an historical landmark, for it forms the basis not only of Plotinus' view of the intelligible structure of being, but also of that of mediaeval Arabian philosophers such as Avicenna. One principle dominates the thought of this philosophical tradition, namely, that plurality is necessary to being, that non-being and otherness are as real as sameness and being [3]. Could a Christian hold that being is essentially multiple? Since this question did not appear to Christian thinkers in quite such a simplified form, they did not find it easy always to answer with a decided negative. The question could be varied, however, and to consider the consequences of a philosophy which could give rise to such a question did not always prove a simple undertaking. No less difficult, and, if anything, more pressing, was the problem of knowing to what extent a Christian could philosophize in Platonic or Neoplatonic ways. To consider such a problem successfully, one would have to establish with precision the frontiers and boundaries which ultimately separate a Greek or Arabian view of God, of the universe and of man from the corresponding view that is native to Christian thought. It was the merit of St. Thomas Aquinas that he saw the fundamental issue involved in this historical meeting between Greek and Christian ideas. His success as an interpreter of Greek and Arabian philosophy is scarcely less important than his eminence as a philosopher. Indeed, the interpreter and the philosopher in St. Thomas are inseparable, and to study the one is always to be indirectly aware of the other.

The problem which commands the decisions of St. Thomas Aquinas is the problem of creation. It is to this problem that he reduces the most fundamental differences between his own philosophical ideas and the ideas of Greek and Arabian philosophers. He has gone to considerable trouble to analyze the different views of Plato or Avicenna and he has shown that their most distinctive characteristics, which are also the characteristics that must be handled prudently by Christian thinkers, center around their conception of the origin of the universe. He has shown what

view of the universe and of God the doctrine
of creation presupposes as well as what view
of creatures it can and indeed must guarantee.
He has shown that there is a metaphysical
context within which the doctrine of creation
belongs and of which it is a natural and inevitable expression. And in the process of thus
showing the economy of ideas surrounding
the doctrine of creation, he has also taken the
occasion to show from what metaphysical
economy and context the doctrines of the
Greeks and the Arabians proceed. He has
shown thereby what must happen to Greek
and Arabian ideas before they can express
adequately the philosophical doctrines of
Christian thinkers.

The experiences of St. Thomas Aquinas
with the problem of creation are thus both
philosophically and historically crucial. They
enable us not only to have a better understanding of the events that occupied the thirteenth century, but also to appreciate more
clearly those ideas of Greek and Arabian

philosophers which many of us have successfully forgotten. I say *successfully,* because
some interpreters of Greek philosophy proceed as though Greek thinkers were less perfect models of what Christian thinkers were to
be in a more perfect way. The relations of
Aristotle to St. Thomas Aquinas are a case in
point. There are, in reality, two questions involved in these relations. There is the philosophical question, and the historical question;
and our view of the relations themselves will
differ according as we adopt the historical or
philosophical level of discussion. The philosopher who is also a disciple of St. Thomas
Aquinas may well say that "the doctrine of
Aristotle did not bear its purest fruit except in
the mind of St. Thomas Aquinas. Not only
did St. Thomas Aquinas correct and develop
Aristotle, he also transfigured him in placing
him in the higher light of faith and theology.
But since he has always remained absolutely
faithful to all the principles of Aristotle, one
may say that he is much more purely Aristo-

telian than Aristotle" [4]. Such a judgment, rich in philosophical vision, leaves the historical question untouched, for we have still to determine the meaning which the historical Aristotle would have if he did not have the advantage of being seen in the context of the mind of St. Thomas Aquinas. And we are impelled to this conclusion not only by the various criticisms levelled by St. Thomas against Aristotle, but also by the fact that an Aristotle who is an incipient Thomist is, in the long history of Aristotelian commentators, a unique phenomenon.

Permit me to introduce at this point an historical digression. Those who study the history of mediaeval thought find it natural and convenient to look upon Greek philosophy as the predecessor of mediaeval philosophy. No one can deny that Christian thinkers are indebted to Greek and Arabian philosophers for many of their ideas. But the habit of looking at Greek thought as a predecessor of mediaeval thought has had an unfortunate effect both on our view of Greek philosophy and of mediaeval philosophy. For so long as the Greeks are considered as predecessors, they have a meaning as philosophers only in relation to those ideas of which they are predecessors. The only trouble is that these same Greek philosophers cannot have such a meaning for themselves. To look at them as predecessors of Christian thought is, in part, to look at them out of focus. It is to look at them from a standpoint which is not their own. It is perfectly true that they can be recognized as being on the way to the ideas of Christian thinkers. For example, it has been held, and with eminent historical justice, that the Greeks were on the way to solving the problem of the origin of being. The only question is, from what point of view one must look at the Greeks in order to be able to say that this was the direction of their efforts. It almost looks as though we are committing ourselves to saying that we must first read history backward in order to read it forward.

That is like saying that one must look at Greek philosophy with Christian eyes in order to understand what the Greeks were talking about. At this rate it becomes a mystery to know what the Greeks thought of themselves.

The question is really a serious one. If we must assume the philosophical present in order to understand the philosophical past, are we not eliminating from the past exactly that significance which it had for itself? Let us suppose that Aristotle was on the way to monotheism and to the doctrine of creation. Since it is assumed that he did not quite reach these doctrines, are we not suppressing the question as to the doctrines which he actually did reach if we interpret his thought as being a failure to reach what he did not reach? If, in fact, Aristotle did not know the doctrine of creation, we cannot interpret his philosophy as though he intended it and did not reach it or as though the fact that he did not reach it really left his philosophy incomplete. *We* may think that he ought to have reached it and that, assuming our interpretation of his principles, he was falling short of what he ought to have done. It is only in relation to how we see the universe that the philosophy of Aristotle can be held to be incomplete or even misguided. Now Aristotle could not take such a view of himself. Hence, in interpreting him, we cannot give him either the advantage or the disadvantage of philosophical ideas that he did not have and could not use; for if we do this, we shall simply eliminate the philosophical experience of Aristotle in the process of endowing him with a share in philosophical truth. In short, our very view of the philosophy of Aristotle must make an effort to see his problems without coloring them by answers which he did not know. For even if we were to grant that St. Thomas is the acme of Aristotelianism, we must still recognize that there is a difference between a thinker who has a problem and knows the answer and another thinker who has the same problem and does not know the answer. And the difference is not only negative, it is also positive. For these thinkers have different views of their problems as problems precisely because one of them has an answer, and the other not. I am suggesting, therefore, that the answers which a Christian thinker gave to the metaphysical problems of Aristotle can both help and hinder us. They can help us in order to discover the truth, and even to discover that truth which an Aristotle may have wanted to reach but did not. But they can also hinder us, for philosophical answers not only solve problems, they also suppress problems. It is more than possible that Christian answers to the problems of Greek philosophy have in reality suppressed many of the difficulties of Greek philosophers [5]. Let me go even a step farther. It is also possible that Greek thinkers were forced to formulate theories to explain problems that actually do not exist in a Christian world. This is not only a possibility, it is also a fact: the doctrine of emanation is such a theory. It is a fact, however, which has a peculiar significance for those who study mediaeval philosophy. For what mediaeval thinkers experienced in Greek and Arabian philosophers was not simply a number of problems inadequately, or even badly, solved, or a number of principles inadequately understood; they experienced also those metaphysical theories which were the counterpart of the view, however inadequate, that the Greeks and Arabs had of their own principles. That these theories were wrong, because based on erroneous metaphysical intuitions, did not make matters easier for thirteenth century thinkers who were in the process of learning the difficult language of philosophy.

## II

The philosopher who does not recognize such possibilities can easily fail to profit by the experiences of philosophers, and the historian who does not recognize them can easily fall victim to his own historical method. Unfortunately, he may also so misinterpret both Greek and Christian thought as to render the one as well as the other not only self-contradictory but also radically unintelligible. There is such an antithesis between a philosophical and historical misinterpretation of this kind and the scrupulous care that St. Thomas Aquinas has taken in discussing his own historical relations to Greek philosophy, that it will serve as a very suitable introduction to St. Thomas' relations to the Greeks if I consider at this point the thesis recently proposed by Professor Arthur Lovejoy in his James Lectures at Harvard University [6]. These lectures contain the story of what Professor Lovejoy considers to be a great metaphysical contradiction begun by Plato, continued and perfected by Aristotle and Plotinus, and made an integral part of Christian thought by such thinkers as St. Augustine and St. Thomas Aquinas. Professor Lovejoy considers exactly that problem which gives to the philosophy of St. Thomas Aquinas precisely that historical significance which I think it has. What he says is thus an excellent point of departure for the problem of the relations of St. Thomas to the Greeks.

Professor Lovejoy borrows from Whitehead the famous saying that "the safest general characterization of the European philosophical tradition is that it consists in a series of footnotes to Plato" [7]. Only, Professor Lovejoy sees two conflicting major strains in Plato. There is a cleavage and an opposition between what he calls otherworldliness and this-worldliness. By otherworldliness he means, not any preoccupation with a future life, but rather a definite view of the universe in itself. This Platonic otherworldliness considers that the world of sense is mutable and "an ever-shifting phantasmagoria of thoughts and sensations," without substance, unstable, relative and elusive. We must turn away from the world of sense and from the life of sense if we are to discover that higher realm of being which is the worthy object of our contemplation. The otherworldly view of this world consists in calling it unreal or illusory. Of course, the otherworldly philosopher is left with a contradiction on his hands, for the world which he says is unreal somehow is [8]. With the famous doctrine of the Idea of the Good in the *Republic,* Plato becomes "the father of otherworldiness in the West" [9]. Those who have caught a glimpse of the Idea of the Good turn to it completely and just as completely ignore this world's business.

Considered as a perfect being, the Idea of the Good was, according to Lovejoy, the God of Plato [10]. Now this God is absolutely self-sufficient. "The fullness of Good is attained once for all in God; and the 'creatures' add nothing to it. They have from the divine

point of view no value; if they were not, the
universe would be none the worse" [11].
Plato himself does not draw this conclusion.
But the conclusion is implied in the doctrine
of Plato. This implication in the doctrine of
Plato is the "primary source of that endlessly
repeated theorem of the philosophic theologian that God has no need of the world and
is indifferent to it" [12]. Here is a God who
is self-contained in His goodness and absolutely indifferent to what goes on in the world.

Now, if Plato had stopped here, the history of European thought would have been
different from what it was. But the most nota-
ble fact about the historic influence of Plato
is "that he did *not* merely give to European
otherworldliness its characteristic form and
phraseology and dialectic, but that he also
gave the characteristic form and phraseology
and dialectic to precisely the contrary tend-
ency—to a peculiarly exuberant kind of this-
worldliness. For his own philosophy no sooner reaches its climax in what we may call the

otherworldly direction than it reverses its course" [13]. For the same God who was self-sufficient and self-contained had also to be the cause of the existence of this world. "The self-same God who was the Goal of all desire must also be the source of the creatures that desire it" [14].

Let us clarify this second phase of Plato's thought by asking with Professor Lovejoy two questions. Why is there any world of becoming in addition to the eternal world of Ideas and the Idea of the Good? Secondly, "what principle determines the number of kinds of being that make up the sensible and temporal world?" [15]. As to the first question, the reason why the universe exists is because God is good and without envy. A self-sufficient God could not be envious of anything. And it is here that Plato's boldness as well as his contradiction begins. "The concept of Self-Sufficing Perfection, by a bold logical inversion, was— without losing any of its original implications —converted into the concept of a Self-Tran-

scending Fecundity. A timeless and incorpo-
real One became the logical ground as well as
the dynamic source of the existence of a
temporal and material and extremely multiple
and variegated universe. The proposition that
—as it was phrased in the Middle Ages—
*omne bonum est diffusivum sui* here makes its
appearance as an axiom of metaphysics" [16].
At this point the trouble begins. "With this
reversal there was introduced into European
philosophy and theology a combination of
ideas that for centuries was to give rise to
many of the most characteristic internal con-
flicts, the logically and emotionally opposing
strains, which mark its history—the conception of (at least) Two-Gods-in-One, of a
divine completion which was yet not complete
in itself, since it could not be itself without
the existence of beings other than itself and
inherently incomplete; of an Immutability
which required, and expressed itself in,
Change; of an Absolute which was nevertheless not truly absolute because it was related,

at least by way of implication and causation, to entities whose nature was not its nature and whose existence and perpetual passage were antithetic to its immutable subsistence" [17]. Professor Lovejoy is not exactly impressed by the dialectic which leads Plato to this conclusion, but it had a history. "The dialectic by which Plato arrives at this combination may seem to many modern ears unconvincing and essentially verbal, and its outcome no better than a contradiction; but we shall fail to understand a large and important part of the subsequent history of ideas in the West if we ignore the fact that this dual dialectic dominated the thought of many generations, and even more potently in mediaeval and modern than ancient times" [18].

Let us reserve comment and pass on to the second question. If it be asked how many kinds of temporal and imperfect beings must this world contain? the answer is, "*all* possible kinds" [19]. This is understood in the strictest possible sense and becomes what Professor Lovejoy calls the principle of plenitude according to which the Platonic universe contains realized within itself all possibilities. It is a *full* universe in the sense that in it all that can be, actually is. This applies not only to a fullness according to which the universe contains the whole range of the different kinds of things, but also to a fullness according to which "no genuine potentiality of being can remain unfulfilled" [20]. This means "that the extent and abundance of the creation must be as great as the possibility of existence and commensurate with the productive capacity of a 'perfect' and inexhaustible Source, and that the world is better the more things it contains" [21].

By this conclusion, Plato has, according to Professor Lovejoy, contradicted his own otherworldliness. For, "since a God unsupplemented by nature in all its diversity would not be 'good,' it follows that He would not be divine. . . . The world of sense could no longer, except by an inconsistency, be adequately described as an idle flickering of insubstantial shadow-shapes, at two removes from both the Good and the real. . . . The shadows were as needful to the Sun of the intellectual heavens as the Sun to the shadows; and though opposite to it in kind and separate from it in being, their existence was the very consummation of its perfection. The entire realm of essence, it was implied, lacked what was indispensable to its meaning and worth so long as it lacked embodiment" [22]. In other words, God or the Good had to produce the universe in order to remain good and in order to remain divine. There was some sense in which God would not be perfect unless He gave existence to all possible beings; unless, therefore, His goodness extended to and actualized everything that could be; unless the universe were a full chain of being containing within itself all created possibilities, from the highest to the lowest, actually realized. Furthermore, this explanation of the divine goodness "is not the consequence of any free and arbitrary act of choice of the personal Creator in the myth; it is a dialectical necessity. The Idea of the Good is a necessary reality; it cannot be other than what its essence implies; and it therefore must, by virtue of its own nature, necessarily engender finite existents. And the number of kinds of these is equally predetermined logically; the Absolute would not be what it is if it gave rise to anything less than a complete world in which the 'model,' i.e., the totality of the ideal Forms, is translated into concrete realities. It follows that every sensible thing that is, is because it—or at all events, its sort—cannot but be, and be precisely what it is. This implication, it is true, is not fully drawn out by Plato himself; but since it is plainly immanent in the *Timaeus,* he thus bequeathed to later metaphysics and theology one of the most persistent, most vexing, and most contention-breeding problems. The principle of plenitude had latent in it a sort of absolute cosmical determinism which attains its final systematic formulation and practical application in the *Ethics* of Spinoza" [23].

With Neoplatonism, the doctrine of Plato and Aristotle is fully organized into a coherent scheme of things. More specifically, the Neoplatonic theory of emanation is, for Professor Lovejoy, "an attempt at a deduction of the necessary validity of the principle of plenitude" [24]. That is to say, in Plotinus more than in Plato "it is from the properties of a rigorously otherworldly, and a completely self-sufficient, Absolute, that the necessity of the existence of this world, with all its manifoldness and its imperfection, is deduced" [25]. The theory of emanation explains how the many are generated from the One in a descending and hierarchical order until all possibilities are realized even unto the last and the least. Reality is thus an immense and continuous span embodying one life that proceeds from the outpouring of the transcendent Good. From the One to Intelligence, from Intelligence to Soul, from Soul to living and non-living substances, and from these to matter, reality stretches like Homer's golden chain without a link missing and without a link out of place. Nor must we suppose that the One gave forth of its life by any choice of its will or by any deliberation. It is as necessary to the One to overflow and to generate this universe as it is for it to be good. The universe must be and it must be as it is: only such a universe can proceed from the goodness of the Plotinian God. Necessity reigns supreme, for it rules even the divine life.

Let me note at this point the essentials of Professor Lovejoy's theory before turning to its further application and development in mediaeval thought. The God of Plato and Plotinus is involved in contradiction. On the one hand we are asked by these Greek philosophers to believe that God as a perfect goodness is self-sufficient and free of any need to go outside Himself in order to be perfect. Being the very essence of goodness, He lacks nothing; lacking nothing, He seeks nothing;

seeking nothing, He can remain radically and completely self-sufficient. The universe not only adds nothing to His perfection, it scarcely contains any perfection within itself. It is like an illusion and a darkness from which one ought to flee. And yet, having come thus far, having driven the universe into the desolation of outer darkness, these same Greek philosophers proceed to reverse themselves and to make of their self-sufficient and impassible God the necessary source of the universe. And what a universe! Not only does God create it, God must create it; not only does it contain some perfection that creatures can have, it contains all possible created perfection. Far from being one of many worlds that God might have chosen, it is *the* world which He must produce, and produce so necessarily that He is as forced to produce it as He is to be Himself. It is the best possible world, it is the only possible world, for it is the world which is full of all possibilities: God's goodness has exhausted itself in making it. This universe, far from being a penurious stranger at the banquet of the divine goodness is in reality an honored guest. Or so Plato and Plotinus will have us believe. But what has happened to that philosophy of otherworldliness? to that self-sufficient Good who holds Himself aloof from the universe? to that spurning of the world and everything in it as worthless and passing and illusory? Strange illusion indeed, if it is eternally honored by the divine goodness.

It seems that we must choose. Either God is a self-sufficient Good and free to create or not to create, in which case the universe need not be and, if it is, is only one of many possibilities freely chosen and just as freely created. Or God cannot be perfectly good unless He creates, and more specifically, unless He creates everything that can be, until His goodness has reached every creature, however insignificant. I say we must choose: either a God who is a self-sufficient Good and has little interest and certainly no profit in an impoverished universe, or a God whose goodness compels Him to produce the best of all possible worlds and who cannot be good until and unless He does so.

When he turns to Christian thought, Professor Lovejoy discovers anew this Platonic dilemma. We shall now witness in Christian thinkers the conflict between otherworldliness, produced by the self-sufficiency of the divine goodness, and this-worldliness, produced by the worldliness of God Himself. Let us pass over St. Augustine and Dionysius, the mysterious pseudo-Areopagite, who handed this dilemma on to Christian thought; let us pass over Abelard, whose position in this problem was very ambiguous [26], and let us come to the man whom Professor Lovejoy calls "the greatest of the Schoolmen" [27]. Through the example of St. Thomas Aquinas Professor Lovejoy hopes to show "both the embarrassment which this internal strain in the traditional doctrine caused him and the ingenious but futile logical shifts to which it compelled him to resort" [28]. St. Thomas is first of all quoted as follows:

"Everyone desires the perfection of that which for its own sake he wills and loves: for the things we love for their own sakes, we wish . . . to be multiplied as much as possible. But God wills and loves His essence for its own sake. Now that essence is not augmentable or multipliable in itself but can be multipled only in its likeness, which is shared by many. God therefore wills things to be multiplied, inasmuch as He wills and loves His own perfection. . . . Moreover, God in willing Himself wills all the things which are in Himself; but all things in a certain manner pre-exist in God by their types (*rationes*). God, therefore, in willing Himself wills other things. . . . Again, the will follows the understanding. But God in primarily understanding himself, understands all other things; therefore, once more, in willing Himself primarily, He wills all other things" [29].

On this passage Father Rickaby had already commented as follows: taken by itself, it "might seem to argue that God wills the existence of all things, that He understands as possible, and that He necessarily wills the existence of things outside Himself, and so necessarily creates them" [30]. Professor Lovejoy goes farther, indeed much farther. "Not only might the passage mean this; it can, in consistency with assumptions which Aquinas elsewhere accepts, mean nothing else" [31]. In fact, "all possibles 'fall under an infinite understanding,' in Spinoza's phrase, and, indeed, belong to its essence; and therefore nothing less than the sum of all genuine possibles could be the object of the divine will, i.e., of the creative act" [32]. This means that St. Thomas Aquinas holds the doctrine, or at least holds principles which give rise to the doctrine, that God knows and also wills the existence of all possibles so that his universe is as full and his God as necessitated as were the universe and the God of Plotinus. However, there are difficulties. "But Thomas cannot, of couse, admit this; he is under the necessity of affirming the freedom of the absolute will; *necesse est dicere voluntatem Dei esse causam rerum, et Deum agere per voluntatem, non per necessitatem naturae, ut quidam existimaverunt.* Consequently the creation must be restricted to a selection from among the Ideas" [33].

Now how does St. Thomas avoid the dilemma which thus threatens to overtake him? Here is Professor Lovejoy's view of the matter: "In order to exclude necessity without excluding goodness from the divine act of choice, Thomas first introduces a distinction— which is almost certainly the source of the similar one in Leibniz and Wolff—between absolute and hypothetical necessity: the will of God, though it always chooses the good, nevertheless chooses it 'as becoming to its own goodness, not as necessary to its goodness' " [34]. Professor Lovejoy's verdict on this distinction is extremely unfavorable: "This is a distinction which will not bear scrutiny; to choose other than the greater good would be, upon Thomistic principles, to contradict both the notion of the divine essence and the notion of volition; and in any case, the argument grants that the greater good, which here implies the greatest sum of possibles, is in fact chosen" [35].

St. Thomas proceeds farther and adds "a highly characteristic piece of reasoning" [36]. Its result is to deny the principle he has already accepted. Professor Lovejoy again quotes St. Thomas as follows:

"Since good, understood to be such, is the proper object of the will, the will may fasten on any object conceived by the intellect in which the notion of good is fulfilled. Hence, though the being of anything, as such, is good, and its not-being is evil; still, the very not-being of a thing may become an object to the will, though not of necessity, by reason of some good which is attached to it; for it is good for a thing to be, even at the cost of the non-existence of something else. The only good, then, which the will by its constitution cannot wish not to be is the good whose non-existence would destroy the notion of good altogether. Such a good is none other than God. The will, then, by its constitution can will the non-existence of anything except God. But in God there is will according to the fullness of the power of willing, for in Him all things without exception exist in a perfect manner. He therefore can will the non-existence of any being except Himself, and consequently does not of necessity will other things than himself" [37].

According to this conclusion, therefore, "though the divine intellect conceives of an infinity of possible things, the divine will does not choose them all; and the existence of finite things is therefore contingent and the number of their kind is arbitrary" [38].

But Professor Lovejoy will not grant that this conclusion is legitimately reached. "But the argument by which the great Schoolman seeks to evade the dangerous consequences of his other, and equally definitely affirmed, premise is plainly at variance with itself as well as with some of the most fundamental principles of his system. It asserts that the existence of anything, insofar as it is possible, is intrinsically a good; that the divine will always chooses the good; and yet that its perfection permits (or requires) it to will the non-existence of some possible, and therefore good, things" [39]. Now precisely, what Professor Lovejoy wants to know is how St. Thomas Aquinas can accept at one and the same time both the Platonic principle of plenitude, according to which creation is full of all possibilities, and the assertion that the divine will freely chooses only some of an infinite number of creatable possibilities. If the divine goodness required God to produce all possible beings, how can St. Thomas say that this same God freely chooses to create some possible beings?

Furthermore, Professor Lovejoy finds St. Thomas saying that multiplicity and variety are necessary in creation in order that the perfect likeness of God might be found in things according to their measure. St. Thomas further says that "the perfection of the universe therefore requires not only a multitude of individuals, but also of diverse kinds, and therefore diverse grades of things" [40]. Professor Lovejoy comments: "It must be patent to the least critical reader of this passage that here, once more, the Angelic Doctor avoids embracing the principle of plenitude in its unqualified form only by an inconsequence, since he, like every orthodox theologian, held that the divine power extends not simply to 'various' but to an infinity of effects. The substitution of 'many' for 'all possible' was a manifest drawing back from the conclusion which the premises not only permitted but required" [41]. Hence the following conclusion on St. Thomas: "Returning to the author of the *Summa Theologica,* his position with respect to the principles of plenitude and continuity may now be summed up. He employs both freely as premises, we have seen, whenever they serve his purpose; but he evades their consequences by means of subtle but spurious or irrelevant distinctions when they seem to be on the point of leading him into the heresy of admitting the complete correspondence of the realms of the possible and the actual, with the cosmic determinism which this implies" [42]. Nor was St. Thomas alone in this inconsequence, for "all orthodox mediaeval philosophy, except the radically anti-rationalistic type, was in the same position" [43].

Thus far Professor Lovejoy. I have quoted him at some length because his thesis is of considerable importance, both historical and philosophical. And more particularly, its relevance to any discussion of the relations between St. Thomas and the Greeks ought to be perfectly obvious. But its bearing on the present discussion must be determined with exactness. That I shall disagree with Professor Lovejoy is not nearly as important as are the reasons for that disagreement. Let me agree first of all, that what Professor Lovejoy calls a contradiction and a confusion is nothing less than that. The difficulty begins, however, when we try to locate that contradiction historically. For, if I am not mistaken, Professor Lovejoy has given an elaborate report of events that never happened. If we limit ourselves to the chief actors in this discussion, namely, Plato, Plotinus and St. Thomas Aquinas, I say that Professor Lovejoy has described a contradiction in which they are made to share, but which they have not produced. And they have not produced it because none of them ever held that combination of ideas which leads to the position from which, as we are told, St. Thomas Aquinas can escape only by an inconsequence. For the contradiction is in reality much more contradictory than Professor Lovejoy supposes. In fact, it is only by looking at the contradiction itself in a confused and vague sort of way that we could ever suppose it to have been as such an historical reality.

The contradiction, in fact, is ultimately based on two irreducible notions of goodness having two irreducible and opposed consequences. According to the one, God, as the essence of goodness, is self-sufficient and therefore does not have to produce any universe. If He does, He does so freely, and a world so produced is entirely contingent. The goodness of God is the source of His self-sufficiency, His freedom and the radical contingency of the universe. The second notion of goodness has totally different results. According to this notion, God cannot be the essence of goodness unless He produces all possible worlds or a world of all possibilities. God is now completely necessitated to act as He does and to produce what He does in order to be good. Necessity and determinism are the correlatives of this second notion of goodness. Quite obviously, a goodness which is self-sufficient and free cannot be a goodness which is determined and necessitated. If one and the same God is described in both ways, we have the contradiction of Professor Lovejoy. But which of these three philosophers—Plato, Plotinus, St. Thomas Aquinas—held the doctrine of a God who was at once free and necessitated? To discuss this question on an historical level, and to attempt to show by an analysis of the texts that none of them ever subscribed to this contradiction, would not be sufficient. It would not be sufficient because it would not enable us to consider the real difficulty that besets Professor Lovejoy's analysis. That difficulty lies in philosophy and in the distinction of philosophical doctrines. Professor Lovejoy, acting as an historian, finds a contradiction because he insists on identifying where he should distinguish and even separate. In brief, he discovers a contradiction vitiating Greek and mediaeval philosophy because he does not, as a philosopher, make those distinctions which are essential to the doctrines which he is studying. Under what he conceives to be the doctrine of creation, he brings together what is in reality a strange philosophical company, and he makes as inhabitants of the same philosophical world thinkers who, as philosophers, never met. It is only because Professor Lovejoy looks at Plotinus and St. Thomas Aquinas in the way that he does that he can see in them what he does.

The most fundamental reason for insisting on this point is that, in the face of the same historical situation, St. Thomas Aquinas has expressed himself in a way which is in decisive disagreement with the philosophical and historical attitude of Professor Lovejoy. The difference is not one according to which, agreeing on the philosophical and historical facts, St. Thomas Aquinas and Professor Lovejoy disagree in their evaluation of these facts. The differences are concerned with the philosophical facts themselves, as well as with

their historical status. If we look at the matter
as St. Thomas does, then what Professor Lovejoy assumes to be the facts in the case are not
even facts at all. For they are facts only if we
concede that that complex of ideas which constitutes the historical contradiction of Professor Lovejoy existed in substantially the same
way in all the philosophers concerned and can
be called in all cases by the name of creation.

Professor Lovejoy attributes the doctrine
of creation indiscriminately to Plato, Plotinus
and St. Thomas Aquinas. A universe that is
produced by emanation is for him a created
universe. He seems to think that a universe
produced in any way, and produced by any
sort of God, is a created universe. The God of
Plato is conceived to be a creator like the God
of St. Thomas Aquinas. The divine goodness
is conceived to be fundamentally the same for
all these philosophers. When they speak of
God as a perfect being, Professor Lovejoy
does not question but what they mean the
same thing. In short, assuming that they agree

in the characteristics which they attribute to God, to the way in which He acts, and to what He produces, Professor Lovejoy proceeds to find Plato, Plotinus and St. Thomas Aquinas in contradiction with themselves. Such a result is as tenable as the assumption upon which it is based. That assumption is Professor Lovejoy's extremely syncretistic notion of creation. Can we find in St. Thomas Aquinas this notion of creation? Can we find in him that contradiction which Professor Lovejoy considers to be its essential characteristic? To seek an answer to such questions is to experience anew St. Thomas' relations to the Greeks; it is also to recapture sufficiently the meaning of the idea of creation in order to allow both to a Plotinus and a St. Thomas Aquinas a greater philosophical integrity than historians sometimes imagine.

### III

Let me point out, first of all, that St. Thomas Aquinas relates three ideas to one another in an inseparable way. God is perfect being. There can be only one perfect being. All other beings that exist require to be created by this being [44]. This is simple, but it is also decisive. From the nature of God as perfect being it follows that there is one and only one God [45], and it follows also that all other beings that exist are created by that God [46]. God possesses all the perfections of existence: nothing of the perfection of being is lacking to Him [47]; He is universally perfect, for He is with the whole power of being [48]. To be is His nature. When we say, therefore, that God is a perfect being, for St. Thomas Aquinas we mean, or we ought to mean, not that God exists with a certain kind of perfection, but that to be without any limitation or defect is His nature. That is why God is one. In other words, monotheism is for St. Thomas a necessary consequence of his concept of God. Since God is perfect as being, in other words, since He is all and completely all that being can be, He can be only one.

We do not always see the implications of these conclusions. Upon the perfection of God so understood, and only so understood, St. Thomas has built his whole theory of the divine causality, the divine liberty, as well as his theory of the contingency of the universe. If God is a necessary being, it is because He is being itself. If all other beings are in any sense produced, they are produced in the ultimately radical sense of being made to be beings. The production itself by which things come into existence, and which is called creation, is a production which gives to things their existence. But notice: it is a production which can function only in a world in which the dependence of things is with respect to their very existence. Now there can be such dependence only in a world in which existence is exclusively and therefore uniquely possessed by God. To be creatures, therefore, is a relation which things can have to God only when God is being itself; or, to put the matter differently, God alone can create, but He can create because He is being [49].

Furthermore, the kind of causality which relates God to the universe, and the conditions of the exercise of that causality, can be shown to depend on the kind of being that God is. How does God will things outside Himself? How does the universe proceed from God? To these questions the answer of St. Thomas is constantly the same. If God is existence itself, such that no perfection of being is lacking to Him, then He is a being whose very perfection frees Him from the necessity of seeking anything outside His own nature and goodness in order to be perfect. He is radically self-sufficient, for He is radically being. Such a God does not have to will the existence of any reality outside Himself. If we accept the premises of St. Thomas Aquinas, we must say that the non-existence of the universe is, strictly speaking, compatible with

the perfection of a God who is infinite being [50]. Since, in fact, the universe cannot
add anything to the perfection of a being that
*is* perfectly and without limitation, it has no
intrinsically compelling reason for existing
and God is driven by no intrinsically compelling reason to produce it. The radical contingency of the universe is a necessary consequence of the nature of the Thomistic God.
Furthermore, the liberty of God to create or
not to create is a consequence of the same conception of the divine being. The God of St.
Thomas Aquinas has to produce nothing outside Himself in order to be perfect. He is
existence itself. For this reason it follows that,
*if* God produces anything outside Himself,
*that* He should produce it, or *what* He produces is absolutely contingent. Neither need
be, and for this reason, both are with complete contingency.

The results of this idea are far-reaching.
Not only, in fact, is any effect of God *ad
extra* radically contingent; in comparison with

God it is also radically imperfect. For not only is it true that the production of any effect *ad extra* adds nothing to the divine goodness; it is also true that the divine goodness can be neither represented completely by its effects, nor completely communicated to them. Because this is true, no created order of goodness is in itself a necessary consequence of the fact that God wills His own goodness. From the standpoint of the divine goodness, there is no such thing as a best possible world. Whether we agree with St. Thomas Aquinas or not, we at least ought to recognize that, since for him, no world need be, strictly speaking no world has a greater absolute claim upon God in comparison with any other world. All possible worlds are—possible worlds. None adds to the divine goodness and none commands the divine will. From such an absolute point of view, every universe is infinitely imperfect. Not only this. When St. Thomas says that there must be variety in the universe in order the better to express the divine perfection, he has already made it clear that every finite way of expressing the divine perfection is infinitely inadequate [51].

We shall miss the whole point of St. Thomas' discussion if we do not notice that this doctrine is intended not only to affirm what St. Thomas considers to be native to Christian thought, but also to deny a view of God and the universe that Christian thinkers could not accept. We are, in fact, at an important crossroad. In discussing various problems on the power of God, on how God wills the universe, on whether all things that can exist do exist, St. Thomas distinguishes between a view according to which the universe proceeds from God through an election of His will, and a view according to which the universe proceeds from God through a necessity of His nature. The opposition is between God acting *per libertatem arbitrii* (through freedom of choice) or *per voluntatem* (through will) and *per necessitatem naturae* (through a necessity or compulsion of nature). In making his own the idea that God acts through a freedom of choice, St. Thomas attributes to Avicenna and Platonism the idea that God acts through a compulsion of His nature [52].

The opposition between St. Thomas and Avicenna is in relation to all the important points of St. Thomas' doctrine of creation. They differ, in fact, on the nature of God, how He acts, His immediate effects, the range of His causality. More explicitly, Avicenna held that inferior creatures were produced through superior creatures. The reason for this was, according to St. Thomas, that Avicenna thought that the immediate effect of a simple unity can be only a unity. It is through the mediation of this unity that multiplicity proceeds from the primal unity. Why this mediated procession of multiplicity from unity? Because Avicenna, Algazel and the author of the *Liber de Causis* assumed that God acted through a necessity of nature; according to which way of acting, from a simple unity only a unity can come. Opposed to this Avicennian view is the doctrine which St. Thomas accepts, according to which multiplicity can proceed immediately from unity because God can contain all things in His knowledge and intellect [53].

We may look at the same thing from a slightly different point of view. What is the source of distinction and multiplication in things? Here again we can notice the opposition between St. Thomas and Avicenna. According to St. Thomas Aquinas, the reason why it is said that one cause must produce one effect is because such a cause has been so determined. Now this is not true in the case of God, and therefore we cannot apply to Him the principle that from a unity only a unity can proceed. Hence we cannot say that because God is absolutely simple, a multiplicity can proceed from Him only through the mediation of beings that fall short of His simplicity. We cannot say this, and thereby is eliminated the opinion of Avicenna, who held that God, in knowing Himself, produced a first intelligence in which there can be found a distinction of potency and act, and from which a still lesser intelligence can proceed. For this idea of Avicenna really makes distinction and diversity in things the product of second causes, and not of God Himself. But according to the Christian view of God, the forms of distinct things are found in the divine mind and, therefore, distinction in the universe is the product of the divine intention and not of second causes [54]. There is, in fact, a chorus of denials before we can arrive at an answer to this question that will satisfy St. Thomas Aquinas. What is the cause of distinction in things? It is not chance, it is not matter, it is not the contrariety of first principles, it is not the order of secondary efficient causes, it is not angels, it is not merit or demerit in creatures. It is the intention of God who wills to give to creatures the perfection that they can receive [55]. For the causality of the God who is a creator extends to all beings as the source of their existence. What Avicenna is really doing, therefore, is limiting the power of God. According to this limitation, the farther we proceed from God, the less we are under His power: plurality and diversity in the universe is thus really a sign of the progressive curbing of God's power as well as a sign of the progressive weakening of the control of intelligibility over being [56]. That is why, in the last analysis, the Avicennian God does not, according to St. Thomas Aquinas, have a proper knowledge of singulars. Like some great astronomer, the Avicennian God can predict the singular by knowing the arrangement of the second causes which produce it. But this does not satisfy St. Thomas Aquinas. For a singular is not produced by bringing together universal forms, just as, if one were to know an eclipse through universal causes, one would be able to locate and to predict such an eclipse, but one would not know a singular event [57]. For St. Thomas Aquinas, on the contrary, God, instead of acting like an astronomer and predicting the position of singulars with mathematical precision and generality, has a proper knowledge of singulars in their singularity because His causality extends immediately to them [58].

We could not be told in any clearer way the differences between the limited and finite God of Avicenna and the infinitely perfect God of St. Thomas Aquinas. The universe of Avicenna contains imperfect and contingent events not simply in the sense that these are finite events; it contains imperfect and contingent events in the sense that these events actually escape the causality of God. There is a sense, therefore, in which contingency in the universe of Avicenna is unintelligible and irrational; for its appearance marks also the progressive limiting of the light and the power of God. We are saying, in fact, that to the extent that there is multiplicity and diversity in the universe, to that extent the ordering of the universe is due to other causes besides God. We are doing this in order not to compromise the pure unity of God. But we must recognize, at least, the impasse to which we have come: we have set up an antithesis between unity and plurality according to which these not only compromise one another, but also are forced to live in isolation from one another in order to avoid the fate of mutual elimination. Such is not, however, the thought of St. Thomas Aquinas. The greatest cause of the contingency of things is for him the divine will. Contingency, instead of being a progressive weakening of the necessary procession of order from the One, is included within the immediate dominion of God over all being [59].

And there are still other differences. If we ask, can God do what He does not do? we cannot give a proper answer to the question unless we notice explicitly that we are eliminating from the discussion the notion of a necessitated God. Thus, among those who erred on the limits of the divine power were to be found the philosophers who said that

God can do only what He does do. This
error belongs "to certain philosophers who
said that God acts through a necessity of
nature." We have already met some of them.
Now if their doctrine were true, and if God
acted through a necessity or a compulsion of
His nature, since nature is determined to one
effect, the divine power could extend only to
those things which it actually makes. Under
these conditions, what God does actually ex-
hausts what He can do because what He does,
He does determinately. In order to free the
power of God from such a determination, St.
Thomas Aquinas now undertakes to show that
God does not, in fact, act through a necessity
of nature. A being that acts through a necessity of nature, far from being God, is a being
which has to be directed to its end. Every
agent acts for an end, because all things seek
the good. But the action of an agent, in order
to be in agreement with its end, must be
adapted and adjusted to it. This can be done
only by some intellect which knows the end

as well as the suitability of that which is related to it. Now the intellect which directs to an end is sometimes joined to the agent acting for an end, as in the case of man. Sometimes the intellect is separated, as is clear in the case of the arrow which tends to a determinate end not through an intellect joined to it, but through the intellect of the man guiding it. Whatever acts through a necessity of nature cannot determine its own end for itself, for that which determines its own end acts through itself, and a being that acts through itself has it in its own power to act or not to act, to be moved or not to be moved. But a being that is moved necessarily does not act through itself, since it is determined to one thing. Hence every being that acts through a necessity of nature must have its end determined by some being that is intelligent. Hence also, that being which acts through a necessity of nature cannot be an independent agent (*principium agens*), since its end is determined for it by another being. The conclusion is inevitable: it is impossible for God to act through a necessity of nature [60]. To come to such a conclusion is once again to eliminate the notion of a God who is finite and determined to act as He does. Having freed the divine power of such a limitation, we can now free God from the present order of things. Since God is omnipotent, anything that does not imply a contradiction lies within His power. There are many things which could exist that do not, i.e., there are many things which God could create which He has not created. Now precisely, so to be able to act is to act through an election of the will and not through a necessity of nature [61].

To eliminate such a notion of the divine nature, power and causality is to eliminate, in reality, a whole philosophical attitude. The Avicennian God acts necessarily, determinately and mediately. The Thomistic God acts intelligently, freely and immediately. Necessity rules the world of Avicenna, and necessity rules the God of Avicenna; and what is not necessary in such a world is accidental and a failure of intelligibility in its progressive descent from the One, which is also its progressive exhaustion. However Avicenna may have reconciled his philosophy with the theology of the Koran, it is true that, in philosophy at least, he held what Professor Lovejoy has called the principle of plenitude in all its rigorousness and with all its necessitarianism. In this sense, Avicenna has expressed in a faithful way the necessitarianism of the philosophy of Plotinus [62]. The importance of this meeting between Avicenna and St. Thomas Aquinas is that St. Thomas has separated himself with extreme care and caution from the various necessitarian elements in the Neoplatonism of Avicenna.

## IV

We may ask, at this point, why any philosopher should come to think as Plotinus and Avicenna did. Provided we understand this question in a sufficiently limited way, the historian has some opportunity of answering it. If we may assume that philosophy as an activity of the intelligence is a constant invitation to the philosopher to purify his vision and to translate that purification into a clearer and more coherent statement of his experience of reality; if we may assume that there is an interior rationale in every philosophical experience, acting at once as a dream and as a norm; if we may assume this, and philosophers are constantly inviting such an assumption, we are justified in seeking a reflection of the vision of a Plotinus in his efforts to be true to it. In this sense, and only in this sense, may the historian seek to lay bare the secrets of philosophers [63].

So limited, our question has some opportunity of being answered. Especially is this

true if we keep in mind what St. Thomas
Aquinas has done on the problem of creation.
Far from conceding that the Greeks or that
Avicenna had a doctrine of creation, St.
Thomas Aquinas implies that their philosoph-
ical views are parts of a coherent total view
which is precisely *not* a doctrine of creation.
If we call this second doctrine necessitarianism, then we may say that for St. Thomas
Aquinas, far from being explanations of the
same world, necessitarianism and creationism
are really explanations of different worlds.
Now to discover the worlds in which philosophers are living is to discover also that which
gives vitality to their thinking. The worlds of
St. Thomas Aquinas and Avicenna are different worlds, and the philosophy of each is at
home in the world of each, but not in the
world of each other. We sometimes look at
their philosophies and forget their worlds.
Perhaps we have become so accustomed to
living in our own world that we have forgotten the appearance and the outlines of

other worlds in which other thinkers thought they were living. St. Thomas Aquinas did not for a moment believe that he was living in the world either of Avicenna or of Plotinus. *That* is the reason why he cannot possibly accept their philosophy; and that also is the reason why he warns his contemporaries to examine the philosophy of Avicenna carefully before subscribing to it, or to principles that come from it, lest perhaps by subscribing to it too readily and too uncritically they should find themselves forced to move into the necessitarian world of Avicenna. But because St. Thomas Aquinas thus sought to avoid both the philosophy of Avicenna and the kind of world which that philosophy was intended to explain, we have a good opportunity of seeing something of the character of that strange world which belonged to Greek and Arabian philosophers and which provoked, and in time compelled, the kind of philosophies that they produced.

The exact point of demarcation is the problem of creation. Does the world exist necessarily? Does God produce the world necessarily? Is this the best possible world? Indeed, is this the only possible world? Does this world contain all produced possibilities? Is this world necessary to the divine goodness? Here are many questions, but, be it noted, these very questions are answered in the affirmative by Plotinus and Avicenna, and in the negative, by St. Thomas Aquinas. The peculiarity of St. Thomas' position is that in answering these questions in the negative, he does not simply think that he has explained one way of expressing the doctrine of creation. The peculiarity of his position lies in this, that to answer these questions in the negative is precisely what constitutes the doctrine of creation. Professor Lovejoy and St. Thomas Aquinas are at this point at odds with one another. Professor Lovejoy thinks that the doctrine of creation is common to ancient Greek and mediaeval Christian thinkers. St.

Thomas Aquinas thinks that the ancient Greeks, Plato and Aristotle included, never arrived at that doctrine [64]. Professor Lovejoy thinks that he can subsume under a doctrine of creation the philosophical theories of Plato and Plotinus; St. Thomas Aquinas thinks that those doctrines are precisely the ones that a theory of creation by nature eliminates. Even at the risk of repetition, let me make the opposition clear. A God who must produce the universe is for St. Thomas Aquinas not a creator. A God who must do what He does and cannot choose to do this or that without violating His goodness is again not a creator. A divine goodness which in order to be good must produce necessarily is not the goodness of a God who is the creator of the universe. A divine goodness which is a necessitated goodness and which therefore is radically incompatible with liberty and self-sufficiency is not the goodness of the Christian God. And finally, the universe which exists necessarily, which must be as it is, which ex-hausts all the possibilities of the divine causality, is not a created universe.

That block of doctrine which describes the necessitated world of Avicenna and Plotinus, and which St. Thomas Aquinas is so concerned to eliminate, is capable of becoming a coherent philosophical whole, as well as a persuasive philosophical whole, within its own world. We have some opportunity of experiencing that world as philosophers, rather than as archeologists, if we make an effort to undo that idea in St. Thomas Aquinas which actually eliminated it. Plato writes in the *Parmenides* that just as we must measure the consequences of an idea when it is present, so we must measure its consequences when it is absent [65]. We can follow such good advice in our present problem. For just as the idea of God as being, self-possessed and therefore uniquely possessed, is the master idea that gives to the thought of St. Thomas Aquinas its philosophical unity and equilibrium, so the absence of that idea, which is also the sacrifice of being to its modes, is the ruling principle of the philosophy of Plotinus. And since we are going from one world to another, let us measure our transition before entering. For the difficulty is not simply to report philosophical facts correctly; it is rather to recognize the meaning of the facts which we are reporting. If the philosophy of Plotinus means anything, it means a perfectly articulated system from which the notion of creation is absent. To go from Plotinus to St. Thomas Aquinas is to go from one world to another; and because each is an eminent guide in his own world, we have only to follow them patiently to see with precision the profound differences between them, and we have only to follow the speculations of St. Thomas Aquinas, who was an expert traveler in the world of Neoplatonism, to see that the idea of creation dominates the differences. And yet an eminent scholar, whose work on Plotinus has contributed much to the elucidation of these frontier differences, can attribute to

Plato a theory of creation and contend that the importance of the idea of creation in the history of philosophy is not evident [66]. Such an historical conclusion threatens to eliminate the philosophical significance of Plotinus, as well as to render the history of philosophy before and after him unintelligible. Rather than surrender to it, we must relate our historical opinions more faithfully to the philosophical thinking that they are reporting. Far from surrendering to it, we are invited by Plotinus and St. Thomas Aquinas to resist it in order to be true to them.

Let us consider, therefore, why a philosopher like Plotinus should profess what has been called the principle of plenitude, and why he should seek to justify it by means of the doctrine of emanation. In the light of the philosophical experiences of St. Thomas Aquinas, the answer is: because such a philosopher has not a theory of creation. The answer is sufficient, but it requires to be explained. A universe that is not created is a universe that never began to be; it is a universe which is naturally and inevitably implied within the nature of reality. The existence of such a universe, which for a St. Thomas Aquinas, is an historical fact, becomes according to this view a metaphysical fact. In a strict sense, the universe of Plotinus, as Professor Gilson has pointed out, is a universe without adventure and without history [67]. It is not even a universe, as though it is one of many possible ones. Reality must include *this* universe as a necessary moment and manifestation of its ultimate nature. In other words, a philosopher who commits himself to the proposition that the universe never began to be, is also committing himself to the proposition that the production of the universe is not the making of *beings,* but the eternal and internal differentiation, through procession, of a reality which is radically immortal. The universe is mysteriously implied within the nature of being and shares with God its eternal community. In thus sharing existence with the universe, God must recognize the universe as His constant companion and as the constant limit of His perfections. However good, however perfect, however free we may now consider God, He is neither so good nor so perfect nor so free that He can be without the universe. He may be the highest being, but since He has not the right to be the only being, He can never be a perfect being because He can never be perfectly being. His goodness, His liberty, His self-sufficiency do not give Him an absolute right to existence because He has not a unique right to existence. If He transcends the universe, there is always in His transcendence an element of flight.

We reach, at this point, what is the central conflict in Plotinus. For since the universe cannot be radically immortal without being divine [68], and since it cannot be divine without infecting the ultimate nature of being with its own limitations, God must flee even the divine mind, which is the order of perfect being [69], in order to flee the finiteness of a world divinized in all its imperfections. From the eternity of the world, therefore, to the eternity of its imperfections, to the complete dismembering of being into the distinctly determined and distinctly received acts of being, to the further eternalizing of these contractions of being, to the transformation of being itself into a prisoner of its modes, so that it is distinctly in as many determinate ways as there are finite possibilities: such is the march of ideas that forces itself upon Plotinus. The old Platonic problem of the one and the many receives its ultimate explanation in this Plotinian metaphysics. But the problem is less a mystery than a scandal, the scandal of a God who must retreat from His own Word in order to retain His unity, no less than the scandal of a divine Word which is so eternally burdened with the imperfections of finiteness that it must descend in order to proceed, and so force the silent and solitary retreat of God in order to stem His descent.

Plotinus elaborates these themes with a philosophical vision whose sureness is exciting and magnificent. He knows to the last detail the sort of world in which he is living. His world is a level and a stage in the divine life which stretches from the loneliness of the One to the darkness of matter. Everything is divine in this all too divine Plotinus, because nothing is created: everything is a form of eternity, because nothing is contingent and temporal— nothing, not even time itself, for time is a weakened eternity, a lesser and exteriorized and dramatized eternity, but eternity none the less [70]. All reality is involved in an eternal process of expressing itself to itself in all its possibilities. Having no history, its one activity is an immobile contemplation which is also a silent recall to the One [71].

A philosopher who is living in such a world cannot but ultimately come to have the philosophy of Plotinus, and a philosopher who has such a philosophy cannot but make God as necessitated a being as Plotinus made his God. Between a world so understood and the philosophical explication of such an understanding there is an adequateness of vision which gives to the philosophy of Plotinus its true greatness. Plotinus must subscribe to all the necessitarian principles that Professor Lovejoy has included in the doctrine of plenitude and in the theory of emanation. The Greeks knew this, or at least, the more they developed the more clearly they recognized it. From Plato to Aristotle and from Aristotle to Plotinus the ultimate relations between essence and being have become clarified, but they have not changed. If Aristotle's great occupation with the continuity of motion seems to be a protest against the abstract immobilism of the Pythagoreans, the Atomists, Parmenides and Plato himself, it is also true that the order of nature and of motion is itself immobilized by the eternal species which are its content and its purpose. If with Aristotle, therefore, we seem to be defining with greater justice a genuine dynamism of nature, it is only to imitate in a less perfect way the circular life of the outer heavens and, through it, the impassible Thought that thinks on itself. Immobilism is still the goal, because the norm, of being. Potentiality and novelty, far from being the mark of a genuine contingency, are something of a stain upon eternity. We have only to attempt to incorporate this world within the immobile principles within which it belongs in order to be well on our way to Plotinus.

Now whatever one may think of such a world and of the philosophers who inhabited it, it ought to be perfectly clear that this world has not the nature of a created world, it is not produced by a God who is a creator, nor is it produced in the way that a creating God would produce anything outside of Himself. In brief, this world of Plotinus is in itself, in the way it was produced, in the God who produced it, radically different from the world of St. Thomas Aquinas. St. Thomas knew that and he said so repeatedly, and that is why he was so anxious to have his contemporaries see it as clearly as he did. Under no circumstances may we thus call this world of Greek and Arabian thinkers a created world, and under no circumstances may we call the God of Greek and Arabian philosophy a creating God.

To answer the contradiction proposed as an historical thesis by Professor Lovejoy resolves itself into allowing to the Greeks and to Christian thinkers their own unique visions of the world. Since the worlds of Plato and St. Thomas Aquinas do not coincide there is no inherent contradiction between goodness and liberty or between liberty and self-sufficiency in their worlds. The God of Plato is not a perfect being since He is neither uniquely or exclusively being. For this reason He cannot possess the liberty and the self-sufficiency of a Christian God. The world of Plato is without origin in the order of existence, and therefore, since it must necessarily be, it has eliminated from existence entirely the possibility itself of not being. The necessitarian emanationism of Plotinus simply erects into a creed and a principle this philosophical experience of Plato. This is one member of Professor Lovejoy's contradiction, and it belongs to Greek philosophy and to Arabian philosophy, but only to them and not to the philosophy of St. Thomas Aquinas.

The world of St. Thomas Aquinas is truly contingent because it neither need be nor need it be what it is, nor is it the only possible world. Being freely produced, it is radically contingent, and because it is radically contingent its finite imperfections do not dismember the perfection of pure being. When the world is contingent, and only when the world is contingent is it possible to conceive of a God who is perfectly and absolutely being; for then it is possible to conceive of a reality that can be by nature uniquely being. Because such a God is possible to Christian thinkers, goodness and liberty in Him and contingency in the universe are compossible. What the universe of Plotinus did not have and could not have, the universe of St. Thomas Aquinas must have, namely, liberty in God and contingency in the world. The Plotinian scandal has ceased to exist. So also has the contradiction of Professor Lovejoy, for Plotinus and St. Thomas Aquinas are not affirming the same philosophical principles nor yet are they denying the same philosophical principles, for they indicate unequivocally that they are living in different worlds. St. Thomas Aquinas was perfectly certain that he would not have the necessitarian world of Plotinus and Avicenna. And he knew to the last detail the reason for his refusal.

But perhaps the problem does not stop here, for it is entirely possible that the misadventures of historians are not as important as the philosophical misadventures of St. Thomas' contemporaries. St. Thomas was showing that the world of Arabian thinkers was not compatible, either in its principles or in its consequences, with the world of Christian thinkers, and he was also explaining why this was true. At the moment when Christian thinkers were trying to become philosophers they were also seeing the different philosophies of Greek and Arabian thinkers. Without in the least intending that they as Christian thinkers could inhabit the world of Greek and Arabian Neoplatonism, they were acting as though they could describe their own world and what went on in it in the way in which the Greeks and the Arabs had described theirs. Now here *was* a contradiction, and it is the significance of St. Thomas Aquinas that he was trying to save his contemporaries from it. Not indeed that they were willingly subscribing to the contradiction, but rather that they did not always see that it was a contradiction to describe the world of Christian thinkers as though it were the world of Plotinus; just as they did not always see that in describing their own world in the language and with the ideas of Neoplatonism, they were forcing upon themselves a world which they certainly would not have accepted. They thus found themselves imprisoned between the world in which they lived and the inadequacy of their philosophical vision. When Avicenna became, as with Henry of Ghent [72], the official metaphysician of a Christian thinker, the cause of philosophy in a Christian world was compromised in the extreme. That compromise need not have existed had the voice of St. Thomas Aquinas been heard. But his voice was not heard, and it is a fact that the compromise did not have long to live. Not indeed because Christian thinkers overcame it, but rather because it overcame them.

## V

Some one hundred years after the death of St. Thomas Aquinas, Petrarch was caught between two sorrows. Both of these sorrows were born from his love of the truth contained by Christian wisdom. The first sorrow was that his beloved Cicero lived too early in history to have been a Christian. Would that he had lived a little later in order that the ideas which he expressed with such noble sentiment might have been freed of their pagan errors and their pagan superstition! Would that he had lived a little later so that his noble mind which was on the way to affirming monotheism, the divine providence and the creation of the world would have found peace in the truths that Christianity professed so clearly and that Cicero himself wanted so much. This was Petrarch's first sorrow, and it is reminiscent of the compassion which St. Thomas Aquinas had for the minds of Aristotle and Averroes. St. Thomas, too, could have a genuine sorrow for the fact that their noble minds should thus suffer in the grasp of error. Here is surely in Petrarch and in St. Thomas the compassion and the charity of a Christian for his fellow man.

But this is not Petrarch's only sorrow. If he felt a deep sorrow because Cicero was not a Christian, he felt also an equally deep, if not deeper, sorrow, because his contemporaries, who were supposed to be Christians and who professed the ideas of Christian thinkers, were philosophizing as though Christianity did not exist. Here they were, these young and supposedly learned Aristotelians, proclaiming every error that Aristotle ever committed and proclaiming it as though it were philosophical truth. At least Cicero did not know better; they did, and their guilt was all the greater and the sorrow of Petrarch all the more acute [73].

This second sorrow of Petrarch is also the spectator of the decline of mediaeval thought and of the emergence of what has been called the modern world. And, be it said, in the realm of ideas this world was modern by as much as it could not learn or forgot, as well as by as much as it ignored or misunderstood. In this it was the logical successor of mediaeval thought itself to the extent that mediaeval thought ignored and misunderstood the ideas of St. Thomas Aquinas. To wish that events might have happened otherwise is to wish to undo what transpired at the end of the middle ages and what was already happening in the thirteenth century itself. So to wish is also to wish the impossible. But perhaps so to wish is to love the intensely human personalities of mediaeval thought sufficiently to make their experiences a part of our own vision. In this sense, while we cannot undo their fate, we can save their efforts and their suffering from oblivion, as well as from having been in vain. So to proceed is to practice an historical friendship that is as intensely mediaeval as it is universally Christian.

## NOTES

1. Alain of Lille, *Anticlaudianus*, Lib. V, cap. 3; (ed. Thomas Wright, *The Anglo-Latin Satirical Poets of the Twelfth Century* 2 vols., London, 1872), vol. 2, p. 350. For a very suggestive study of Alain, cf. J. Huizinga, *Uber die Verknüpfung des Poetischen mit dem Theologischen bei Alanus de Insulis* (Amsterdam, 1932). Alain does not hesitate to use Greek mythology to express the truths of Christian theology, and he goes with astonishing ease from Mt. Olympus to a Christian heaven. Nor is this simply a literary device. The verb *pingere,* to which J. Huizinga calls attention (*op. cit.,* pp. 60-65), is used with such astonishing frequency in the *Anticlaudianus,* that it ought not to go unnoticed. *Pictura* is, in fact, a sort of sensible revelation or theophany, and the Christian poet speaks its language, because he has not yet learned to speak the language of philosophy. Apart from the question of sheer poetic ability, the important difference betwen Alain of Lille and Dante is that the discovery of the philosophy of Aristotle comes between them.

2. "Plinius quoque libro secundo de naturali historia dicit (mundum) numen esse aeternum, immensum, neque genitum neque interriturum unquam. Ex hiis itaque et multis aliis quae afferri possent, nisi prohiberet prolixitas, patet evidenter quod plurimi philosophorum simul cum Aristotele asseruerunt mundum carere temporis principio; quod unius verbi ictu percutit et elidit Moyses: *in*

*principio*. Haec adduximus contra quosdam mod-
ernos qui nituntur contra ipsum Aristotelem et
suos expositores et sacros simul expositores de
Aristotele heretico facere Catholicum; mira caeci-
tate et praesumpcione putantes se limpidius intelli-
gere et verius interpretari Aristotelem ex littera
latina corrupta quam philosophos, tam gentiles
quam catholicos, qui eius litteram incorruptam
originalem graecam plenissime noverunt.

"Non igitur se decipiant et frustra desudent ut
Aristotelem faciant Catholicum, ne inutiliter temp-
us suum et vires ingenii sui consumant et Aristotelem Catholicum constituendo seipsos hereticos
faciendo, et de hiis hactenus." (Robert Grosseteste,
*Hexaemeron,* which I am citing according to the
text of J. T. Muckle, C.S.B., now in preparation.
In the Oxford ms. (Queens College 312), the
reference will be found on fol. 40v, col. 1. I take
this opportunity of thanking Father Muckle for
the use of this text. The opening paragraphs of
the *Hexaemeron* have already been published: Cf.
G. B. Phelan, "An Unedited Text of Robert Grosseteste on the Subject-Matter of Theology," *Revue Néoscolastique de Philosophie,* vol. 36, Feb.
1934, pp. 172-179.)

2a.   Apropos of myth in Plato, it has been said that
"the great charm of Plato is that he binds man to
nothing" C. Bigg, *Neoplatonism* (London: S. P.
C. K., 1895) p. 99.

3.   Plato, *Sophistes,* pp. 257 a, 258 b-c, 259 a-d.
For Plotinus, cf. *Enneads,* V, 1 and VI, 2, of

which both are an elaboration of the categories of being in the *Sophistes* and the second is, in addition, a commentary on the second hypothesis of the *Parmenides* (pp. 142 b-143 a). In view of the *Sophistes,* I accept fully a metaphysical, rather than a logical, interpretation of the *Parmenides.* For a view of the *Parmenides* as a dialectical exercise, cf. Paul Shorey, *The Unity of Plato's Thought* (Chicago: U. of Chicago Press, 1903), pp. 57-60; *What Plato Said* (Chicago: U. of Chicago Press, 1933), pp. 185-193. In an important analysis of Plato's theory of Ideas (*Unity*, pp. 27-40), Professor Shorey minimized considerably the metaphysical aspect of Plato's thought. In the main, for Professor Shorey the Ideas were an impregnable bulwark against all forms of relativism (*op. cit.,* pp. 28-29). While this is without question true, the further contention that any philosophy which assumes an absolute has precisely the difficulties that Plato saw in his own theory of Ideas (*op. cit.,* p. 28), is comforting Emersonian transcendentalism, as well as comfortable skepticism, but it is too vague a view of Plato the metaphysician. On the interpretation of the *Parmenides* and *Sophistes,* cf. Victor Brochard, "La théorie platonicienne de la participation d'après le *Parménide* et le *Sophiste*" *Etudes de philosophie ancienne et moderne,* (Paris: J. Vrin, 1926) pp. 113-150. Cf. also A. Diès, *La definition de l'être et la nature des idées dans le Sophiste de Platon* (2nd ed., Paris: J. Vrin, 1932). On Avicenna, cf. *infra.*

4. J. Maritain, *La philosophie bergsonienne* (2nd ed., Paris: Riviere, 1930), p. 439. For more details, cf. *op. cit.*, pp. 438, 440-441, 443, 445, 452-454. And cp. *Science et Sagesse* (Paris: Labergerie, 1935), pp. 155-156. Maritain has himself indicated the distinction between the historical Aristotle and the intellectual "formality" Aristotelianism: cf. *La philosophie bergsonienne,* pp. 438-439.

5. The problem of the one and the many, for example, such as it was understood by Plato and the Platonic tradition after him, is a problem which does not exist in a Christian world. That a Christian thinker may have other problems, similar or equally serious, is not my present concern. The Platonic problem rests on the assumption that unity *must be* both self-possessed and *necessarily* participated in plurality. The Plotinian theory of emanation is intended to explain how this can be and must be. In a Christian world, between the One and the many there intervenes the creative liberty of God. Whatever other mysteries and problems a Christian may have, he ought not to have the Platonic difficulties of participation: the doctrine of creation has suppressed them. But, by the same token, he ought not to view Plato too much from the standpoint of a Christian world: in that way he can easily miss the whole philosophical effort of Platonism in its own world. And not only will he miss the real Plato, he may also endanger his own ideas by following too uncritically the Platonic metaphysics. I may be permitted to refer to an

earlier discussion of this same point, cf. "Scholasticism and History" *Thought,* vol. XIII, no. 49, June, 1938, pp. 209-216.

6. Arthur O. Lovejoy, *The Great Chain of Being, A Study of the History of an Idea* (The William James Lectures delivered at Harvard University, 1933, Cambridge: Harvard U. Press, 1936). My discussion of this book will be limited to chapters II-III (*op. cit.,* pp. 24-98).

7. *The Great Chain of Being,* p. 24, quoting A. N. Whitehead, without reference. Cf. *Process and Reality* (New York: The Macmillan Co., 1929), p. 63. Dr. Mortimer Adler has suggested, by way of sequel, that he "cannot resist adding that Aristotle wrote most of the footnotes." ("The Crisis in Contemporary American Education," in *The Social Frontier,* Feb., 1939, vol. V, no. 42, p. 142.) This is an excellent sequel, but also an embarrassing one, for as a matter of history there have been perhaps as many Aristotles as there have been footnotes. Hence it is better to insist on the judiciousness of what Dr. Adler has written elsewhere, namely, that "the proper name of no man can be used to circumscribe the truth" (*St. Thomas and the Gentiles,* Milwaukee: Marquette U. Press, 1938, p. 67). This conclusion, of course, leaves entirely open the question that, as a matter of history, some philosophers have been more successful than others in discovering the truth and therefore are better guides in investigating it.

8.  *The Great Chain of Being,* p. 31.

9.  *Ibid.,* p. 39.

10. *Ibid.,* p. 42.

11. *Ibid.,* p. 43.

12. *Ibid.,* p. 43.

13. *Ibid.,* p. 45.

14. *Ibid.,* p. 45.

15. *Ibid.,* p. 46.

16. *Ibid.,* p. 49.

17. *Ibid.,* pp. 49-50.

18. *Ibid.,* p. 50.

19. *Ibid.,* p. 50.

20. *Ibid.,* p. 52.

21. *Ibid.,* p. 52.

22. *Ibid.,* pp. 52-53.

23. *Ibid.,* p. 54. The self-sufficiency of Aristotle's *Unmoved Mover,* according to Lovejoy, cannot be the basis of the principle of plenitude. But if Aristotle seemingly separates himself from Platonism here, he adds a principle of his own, that of continuity, which fused "with the Platonic doctrine of the necessary fullness of the world" (*op. cit.,*

p. 55). Furthermore, while Aristotle is considered to be a representative of clear division and vigorous and rigorous classification, nevertheless, according to Lovejoy, Aristotle "first suggested the limitations and dangers of classification, and the nonconformity of nature to those sharp divisions . . ." (*op. cit.*, p. 58). The principle of continuity, indeed, could be deduced from the principle of plenitude. There remained only the application of the Aristotelian science of classification to the universe to produce a great picture of the world as a *vast chain of being* celebrated in verse by Alexander Pope (*op. cit.*, pp. 58-60).

24. *Ibid.*, pp. 61-62.

25. *Ibid.*, p. 62.

26. On the supposed Spinozism of Abelard, an old interpretation that Professor Lovejoy makes his own, cf. the adverse criticism made long ago by Charles de Remusat, *Abélard* (Paris: Librairie phil. de Ladrange, 1845), vol. 2, pp. 389-401.

27. *The Great Chain of Being*, p. 73.

28. *Ibid.*, p. 73.

29. *Summa contra Gentiles*, I, cap. 75, tr. J. Rickaby, *Of God and His Creatures* (London: Burns and Oates, 1905), p. 57 (quoted by A. Lovejoy, *op. cit.*, pp. 73-74).

30. J. Rickaby, *Of God and His Creatures*, p. 57 (quoted by A. Lovejoy, *op. cit.*, p. 74).

31.  *The Great Chain of Being*, p. 74.

32.  *Ibid.*, p. 74.

33.  *Ibid.*, p. 74. The reference to St. Thomas is *Summa Theologica*, I, q. 19, a. 4. On the last three words of this quotation, Professor Lovejoy adds that they "probably refer chiefly to Abelard" (*op. cit.*, p. 342, note 13). As a guess this is scarcely credible. Avicenna would have been much better, cf. *infra*, note 53.

34.  *Ibid.*, p. 74.

35.  *Ibid.*, p. 74.

36.  *Ibid.*, p. 74.

37.  *Contra Gentiles*, I, cap. 81, tr. J. Rickaby, *Of God and His Creatures*, p. 60 (quoted by A. Lovejoy, *op. cit.*, pp. 74-75).

38.  *The Great Chain of Being*, p. 75.

39.  *Ibid.*, p. 75.

40.  *Contra Gentiles*, II, cap. 45, tr. J. Rickaby, *Of God and His Creatures*, p. 108 (quoted by A. Lovejoy, *The Great Chain of Being*, p. 76). However, while this text is in St. Thomas, it does not appear in Rickaby's translation.

41.  *The Great Chain of Being*, p. 76.

42.  *Ibid.*, p. 81.

43. *Ibid.*, p. 81.

44. *Summa Theologica*, I, q. 44, a. 1.

45. *Summa Theologica*, I, q. 11, a. 3. Cp. *Contra Gentiles*, I. cap. 42 and *Commentum in libros IV Sententiarum Magistri Petri Lombardi* I, dist. ii, q. 1, a. 1.

46. *In II Sent.*, dist. i, q. 1, a. 2, Resp.; *Contra Gentiles*, II, cap. 15; *Expositio in Dionysii De Divinis Nominibus*, cap. V, lect. 1.

47. *Summa Theologica*, I, q. 4, a. 3.

48. *Contra Gentiles*, I, cap. 28.

49. *Contra Gentiles*, II, cap. 21; *Summa Theologica*, I, q. 45, a. 5.

50. Quaestiones disputatae: *De Veritate*, q. XXIII, a. 4; *Summa Theologica*, I, q. 19, a. 3, ad 6; *Contra Gentiles*, I, cap. 81.

51. Quaestiones disputatae: *De Potentia*, q. III, a. 16. A compact but important text. Cp. *De Potentia*, q. III, a. 17, ad 7.

52. In what follows, I am not concerned to give an account of Avicenna's theory of emanation, I wish simply to distinguish it from the doctrine of creation in St. Thomas. On the doctrine itself of Avicenna, cf. A. M. Goichon, *La distinction de l'essence et de l'existence d'après Ibn Sina (Avicenna)* (Paris: Desclée de Brouwer, 1937), pp. 201-334. The Avicenna references in St. Thomas have been collected by A. Forest, *La structure métaphysique du concret selon saint Thomas d'Aquin* (Paris: J. Vrin, 1931), pp. 331-360.

53. "Respondeo dicendum, quod quorumdam philosophorum fuit positio, quod Deus creavit creaturas inferiores mediantibus superioribus, ut patet in *Libro de Causis* (prop. X) ; et in *Metaphysica* Avicennae (Lib. IX, cap. iv), et Algazelis, et movebantur ad hoc opinandum propter quod credebant quod ab uno simplici non posset immediate nisi unum provenire, et illo mediante ex uno primo multitudo procedebat. Hoc autem dicebant, ac si Deus ageret per necessitatem naturae, per quem modum ex uno simplici non fit nisi unum. Nos autem ponimus, quod a Deo procedunt res per modum scientiae et intellectus, secundum quem modum nihil prohibet ab uno primo simplici Deo multitudinem immediate provenire, secundum quod sua sapientia continet universa. Et ideo secundum fidem catholicam ponimus, quod omnes substantias spirituales et materiam corporalium Deus immediate creavit, haereticum reputantes si dicatur per Angelum vel aliquam creaturam aliquid esse creatum; unde Damascenus dicit (*De Fide Orthodoxa,* II, cap. 2): 'Quicumque dixerit Angelum aliquid creare, anathema sit' " (*De Potentia,* q. III, a. 4). The reference to Avicenna is *Metaphysics,* Lib. IX, cap. 4 (ed. Venice, 1508, foll. 104v-105r). For Algazel, cf. *Metaphysics,* I, tr. 5 ; (ed. J. T. Muckle, Toronto: St. Michael's College, 1934, pp. 119-120, 125-126). In the *Liber de Causis,* cf. Prop. IX-X (ed. F. Steele, in *Opera hactenus inedita Rogeri Baconi,* Fasc. XII, Oxford: Clarendon Press, 1935, pp. 169-171). On the misapprehension of thirteenth century Latin writers

concerning the relations of Algazel to Avicenna,
cf. D. Salman, O.P., "Algazel et les Latins"
(*Archives d'hist. litt. et doctr. du moyen âge*, vol.
X, 1935-1936, pp. 203-227).

On the presence of things in God *per
modum scientiae*, which eliminates the Avicennian determinism, cf. *De Veritate*, q. II, a.
4; q. III, a. 1-2; *Summa Theologica*, I. q.
15, a. 1. The presence of multiplicity in God
can cause difficulties if a multiplicity of perfections
has to exist as a determinate plurality. That is not
true for St. Thomas Aquinas for whom God, in
being a perfect being, can possess all the perfections of things in a unique way, that of being.
Hence, the possibility itself of the co-existence of
unity and plurality in God depends on freeing
unity from determination and plurality from imperfection. Both are accomplished by a God who
is being and who is also uniquely so. Because this
is true, we can understand how it is that in a world
in which plurality exists necessarily, pure unity
must transcend being in order to transcend its
necessary limitations and imperfections.

On the question of the relations between unity
and multiplicity, interpreters sometimes attribute to
St. Thomas Aquinas a difficulty that he does not
really have. For example, Mr. Robert L. Patterson,
in his book on *The Conception of God in the
Philosophy of Aquinas* (London: Allen and Un-
win, 1933), has indicated in his abstract that "the
most crucial point of all will be found in the last
three chapters of the third part, where I maintain

that his (*scil.* St. Thomas') attempt to harmonize
the Aristotelian and Christian conceptions of God
breaks down owing to the impossibility of recon-
ciling the multiplicity of objects known and willed
by the Diety with the simplicity of the divine essence" (*op. cit.*, p. 10). If we turn to that discussion (*op. cit.*, pp. 284-364), we find that Mr. Patterson's difficulties arise because he cannot derive
Thomistic conclusions from his own premises. If
we grant that the divine unity can be defined as Mr.
Patterson does (*op. cit.*, pp. 297, 298-299, 336)
then in dealing with the simplicity of a "mere ontological point" (*op. cit.*, p. 299), we shall certainly experience Mr. Patterson's difficulties. Such an
ontological point, however, is much more a mathematical monad than the Thomistic infinite being.
Mr. Patterson has created his own problem. Perhaps if he began with St. Thomas' notion of the
divine unity, he might be able to see the validity
of St. Thomas' conclusions.

54. *Contra Gentiles*, II, cap. 42.

55. *Contra Gentiles*, II, cap. 39-45. These texts are
intimately related to an earlier discussion on the
significant theme that God *ex nullo debito, sed
ex mera liberalitate res in esse produxit* (*ibid.*
cap. 44). *Cp. Contra Gentiles*, I cap. 28, 81, 82;
II, cap. 23-24, 26-31.

56. *Contra Gentiles*, II, cap. 22, 42.

57. *De Veritate*, q. II, a. 5.

58. *Summa Theologica,* I, q. 14, a. 11; q. 44, a. 2. Cp. *In I Sent.,* dist. xliii 43, q. 2, a. 1.

59. *De Veritate,* q. XXIII, a. 5.

60. *De Potentia,* q. I, a. 5.

61. *Contra Gentiles,* II, cap. 23; *Summa Theologica,* I, q. 19, a. 4; *De Potentia,* q. III, a. 5.

62. For Plotinus, cf. Fritz Heinemann, *Plotin* (Leipzig: F. Meiner, 1921); Émile Bréhier, *La philosophie de Plotin* (Paris: F. Alcan, 1928); Ralph W. Inge, *The Philosophy of Plotinus* (3rd ed., 2 vols., New York: Longmans, 1929). For Avicenna, cf. A. M. Goichon, *La distinction de l'éssence et de l'existence d'après Ibn Sina (Avicenna),* pp. 224-244. In a study of the *De Potentia* of St. Thomas, it has been shown how the elimination of this necessitarianism and determinism of Avicenna forms the unifying thread and the main historical occasion of the whole work: cf. M. Bouyges, S.J., "L'idée génératrice du *De Potentia* de saint Thomas" *Revue de Philosophie,* vol. II (May-June, 1931), nos. 2-3, pp. 113-131, 247-268.

63. I realize that in writing this paragraph I am treading on controversial territory. Cf. the discussion between Joseph E. Douglas, S.J., and the present writer in *Thought,* (March, 1939), vol. XIV, no. 52, pp. 120-125. But cf. the sequel to the discussion, *ibid.* (June, 1939), vol. XIV, no. 53, pp. 306-309.

64. The question as to how St. Thomas interpreted Aristotle on the problem of creation, is not an easy one to determine. The difficulty arises because St. Thomas did not always distinguish or care to distinguish the historical from the philosophical issue. The truth of the matter is that he is more interested in making Aristotle useful for the thirteenth century than in determining the exact historical position of Aristotle. Nevertheless, while I am far from pretending that the various groups of texts in St. Thomas on Aristotle's relations to the doctrine of creation, as well as to monotheism, can be harmonized with ease, it is difficult to avoid the conclusion that St. Thomas' omissions and denials really constitute a decisive argument against holding that he attributed the doctrine of creation to Aristotle. "I know," writes Marcel de Corte, "that St. Thomas thinks he can find the idea of creation in Aristotle himself . . ." (*Aristote et Plotin,* Paris: Desclée de Brouwer, 1935, p. 141, note 1). Did St. Thomas really think so? The text of the *Summa Theologica* (I, q. 44, a. 2) does not place Aristotle among those who arrived at the notion of the origin of being cf. É. Gilson, *L'ésprit de la philosophie médiévale,* (Paris: J. Vrin, 1932) vol. 1, pp. 240-242. The text of the *De Potentia* (q. III, a. 5) is admittedly difficult, but it does not attribute to Aristotle any more than to Avicenna. We know already that Avicenna is among St. Thomas' opponents on this question (cp. also *De Potentia,* q. III, a. 4 and 8). But there is one text, at least, in which St. Thomas has categorically de-

nied that Aristotle had a doctrine of creation: "Tertius est error Aristotelis, qui posuit mundum a Deo factum non esse, sed ab aeterno fuisse . . ." (*De Articulis Fidei*, 1; ed. P. Mandonnet, *S. Thomae Aquinatis Opuscula Omnia*, Paris: P. Lethielleux, 1927, vol. III, p. 3). Whatever view on Aristotle we attribute to St. Thomas, we must recognize the historical decisiveness of this conclusion. But since St. Thomas Aquinas appears to have imputed to St. Augustine and to Boethius philosophical ideas that he certainly knew they did not have, the question may be asked whether this is not what he did with Aristotle in those texts in which Aristotle appears to assert creation and monotheism (e.g., *De Substantiis Separatis*, cap. XII; *Opuscula*, ed. P. Mandonnet, vol. II, pp. 119-120).

Interpreters of Aristotle who recognize that there is not a doctrine of creation in him are sometimes puzzled by this fact and consider that Aristotle was not really being true to his principles. Cf. R. Jolivet, *Essai sur les rapports entre la pensée grecque et la pensée chretienne* (Paris: J. Vrin, 1931), pp. 3-88; M. de Corte, *Aristote et Plotin* (Paris: Desclée de Brouwer, 1935), pp. 107-175. But perhaps he was being true to his own understanding of his principles, in the light of his own understanding of reality. The world of Aristotle is ordered only with respect to immobile essences. If the eighth book of the *Physics* is intended to achieve the strict necessitarianism of the conclusion of the *De Generatione et Corruptione* (II, cap.

11), the world of Aristotle is in reality much more rigidly static, and his theory of nature much more *closed*, than is ordinarily supposed by anyone who is trying to save Aristotle rather than to see him in his world. Cf. the general interpretation of Aristotle in J. Chevalier, *La notion du nécessaire chez Aristote et ses prédécesseurs* (Paris: F. Alcan, 1915). Cp. R. Mugnier, *La théorie du premier moteur et l'évolution de la pensée aristotélicienne* (Paris: J. Vrin, 1930). In the *De Potentia* (q. III, a. 17), St. Thomas has urged that the doctrine of the eighth book of the *Physics* is a *necessary* consequence of a view of God in which God was *neither* an infinitely perfect being *nor* a creator.

Whether or not St. Thomas actually thought that the eighth book of the *Physics* was an elaborate *argumentum ad positionem,* Siger of Brabant seems to have attributed to him such a view and to have been considerably annoyed that anyone should not look upon that book as containing authentic Aristotelian doctrine, cf. M. Grabmann, *Neu aufgefundene Werke des Siger von Brabant und Boetius von Dacien* (München: Bayerischen Akademie der Wissenschaften, 1924), pp. 18-20; F. Van Steenberghen, *Siger de Brabant d'après ses oeuvres inédites,* vol. 1 (*Les Philosophes Belges,* vol. XII, Louvain: Institut superieur de philosophie, 1931) pp. 213-215. On the present state of Siger studies, cf. now F. Van Steenberghen, *Les oeuvres et la doctrine de Siger de Brabant* (Bruxelles: Palais des Academies, 1938). Whatever may be the ultimate interpretation of Siger, there are definite limitations which must be placed on the supposed development of his thought in the direction of St. Thomas. It is a little difficult to think of Siger as an "admirer and even a disciple of St. Thomas Aquinas" (*op. cit.*, p. 183). Within the limits of the problem of creation, Siger held a strict necessitarianism and emanationism (*op. cit.*, pp. 127-134) during those very years, i.e., 1271-1277, when he is held to have been developing towards St. Thomas on the question of the intellect (cf., for the chronology, the conclusions of Father Van Steenberghen, *op. cit.*, p. 82). It is true that he held such opinions only *recitando;* but while this may have left his faith intact, it was no less disastrous for the cause of philosophy in a Christian world.

65. Cf. Plato, *Parmenides,* pp. 135 e-136 a.

66. The statements are from Professor Emile Bréhier, as reported in the *Bulletin de la société francaise de philosophie,* 31e année, nos. 2-3 (March-June, 1931), pp. 57-58. On the Platonic demiurgus in the *Timaeus,* cf. the clarifying summary of Paul Shorey, *What Plato Said,* p. 349. It is enough to recognize that we are dealing with a God who is seeking to redeem things from the dominion of chaos and necessity to recognize also that we are not dealing with a creator.

67. E. Gilson, *St. Thomas Aquinas (Lecture on a Master Mind,* Oxford Press, 1935), pp. 6-7.
    I may be permitted to eliminate at this point a possible source of ambiguity. In speaking of the

Greek and Neoplatonic world as never having begun to be, I am concerned with a beginning in the order of being, not in the order of time. In this sense a universe which is created from all eternity is still a universe which begins to be. In this sense also, a universe which does not begin to be is indestructible and immortal with respect to its very being. The nature of reality as including within itself a universe unoriginated and immortal in this same sense is the common problem of Greek philosophy.

68. *Enneads*, V, 1, 6; V, 6, 5; VI, 7, 7. Cp. the interesting criticism that Plotinus levels at Aristotle, *Enneads*, IV, 7, 8[5].

69. Cf. *supra*, note 3 and cp. the recent discussions of J. P. Fitzpatrick, S.J., and B. J. Muller-Thym in *Proceedings of the American Catholic Philosophical Association*, (December, 1938) vol. XIV, pp. 169-191.

70. Cf. *Enneads*, III, 7 and the important discussion of Jean Guitton, *Le temps et l'éternité chez Plotin et saint Augustin* (Paris: Boivin et Cie, 1933).

71. Cf. *Enneads*, III, 8. This treatise is not simply an extension of Aristotle's theory of contemplation; it is also a transformation of Aristotle's philosophy of nature into a doctrine of static contemplation. The order of nature is a weakened and even a menial order of contemplation, but it expresses no less rigidly the eternal changelessness of

being. Who shall say that Plotinus was unjust in such a transformation?

72.   Cf. the important study of Jean Paulus, *Henri de Gand, essai sur les tendances metaphysiques* (Paris: J. Vrin, 1938).

How far Latin thinkers could go in the direction of Avicenna can be seen from the anonymous *De causis primis et secundis,* written probably in the early thirteenth century: cf. the edition of the text and the study on "Latin Avicennism" in R. de Vaux, *Notes et textes sur l'avicennisme latin,* (Paris: J. Vrin, 1934). The case of St. Albert the Great is notoriously puzzling. In my dissertation I indicated, in a general way, his Avicennian interpretation of Aristotle's psychology—an interpretation which leaves the Platonic sympathies of St. Albert intact (cf. A. C. Pegis, *St. Thomas and the Problem of the Soul in the Thirteenth Century,* Toronto: Institute of Mediaeval Studies, 1934, pp. 77-120). But the Avicennian sympathies of St. Albert go farther than this. In a forthcoming work, Dr. B. J. Muller-Thym will show the Neoplatonic conception of being and intelligence that St. Albert accepted and handed on to Meister Eckhart (cf. B. J. Muller-Thym, *The Establishment of the University of Being in Meister Eckhart,* New York: Sheed and Ward, announced for October, 1939). Finally, we may notice that the position of St. Albert on creation is far from clear. His texts are not in agreement, and the problem appears ultimately to be, not whether he rejects emanationism, but whether he can do so for philosophical reasons. Cf. *Liber de Causis et Processione Universitatis*, I, 6 (*Opera*, ed. Borgnet, vol. X, p. 372) ; *De Intellectu et Intelligibili*, I, 1, 5 (ed. cit., vol. IX, p. 484) [the view of the philosophers that *ab uno simplici non est nisi unum*] contra: *Sum. Theol.*, P. II, Tr. 1, q. 3, ad 1 (ed. cit., vol. XXXII, p. 26). Between these texts there lies the idea of St. Albert that the philosophers did not know *creatio*: cf. *Sum. Theol.*, P. I, Tr. 13, q. 53, mem. 1 (ed. cit., vol. XXXI, p. 544). Cp. also *In II Sent.* dist. i A, a. 5; dist. i B, a. 10; dist. i C, a. 12 (ed cit., vol. XXVII, pp. 18, 27, 33-34). But cf., on the whole question, the discussion and references in M. Grabmann, *Mittelalterliches Geistesleben*, Band II (München: Max Hueber Verlag, 1936), pp. 287-312. For a recent Avicennian interpretation of St. Albert, cf. the interesting article of William E. Dooley, "St. Albert: A Point of Departure," *The Modern Schoolman*, vol. XVI, no. 4 (May, 1939), pp. 83-87.

73.  Cf. Petrarch, *De Sui Ipsius et Multorum Stultitia*, IV, (ed. L. M. Capelli, Paris: Librairie H. Champion, 1906), pp. 39ff. Cp. St. Thomas, *Contra Gentiles*, III, cap. 48.